THE SOUND OF WHAT BOTHERS ME

THE SOUND OF WHAT BOTHERS ME

THOMAS CALDER

Thomas Calder

Copyright © 2021 by Thomas Calder

All rights reserved. No part of this book may be reproduced in any manner whatsoever without written permission except in the case of brief quotations embodied in critical articles and reviews.

First Printing, 2021

For my loves.

THE SOUND OF WHAT BOTHERS ME

A collection of offerings

THOMAS CALDER
THE SOUND OF WHAT BOTHERS ME
Copyright © 2021 by THOMAS CALDER
For information contact :
Thomasccalder@gmail.com
+61431702 792

#1

We wearily
    Possess the results
    Of our labour
    With restless grip
    While
    Already reaching
    For more.
    Compulsively,
    We refocus the gaze
    Of our needing
    And power ever forward,
    Piling productiveness
    Atop of success
    In the hope of burying
    Our hardships.
    We are throwing the wrong things
    Away
    And without even
    Getting to know them.
    Let's change our minds,
    Be still,
    Do nothing for prestige,
    Have patience,
    Sleep well,
    Be generous
    And
    Sing together
    When it's someone's special day.

The world
        Is a ridiculous idea.
        I spend days
        Trying to wake up
        And evenings
        Losing sleep.
        Is it,
        Man pushing himself?
        Or;
        Himself, pulling Man?
        Himself, being;
        The idea of what Man should amount to,
        And man being;
        Its own inadequate vessel.
        We,
        As the people we inhabit now,
        Work
        For holidays and shiny things,
        On behalf of
        The people we will become,
        Assuming
        They will have similar interests.
        There are too many things
        To think about.
        No wonder
        We are tired,
        And cannot sleep

Bad faith,
    And
    The balance of my heart.
    A statistical smear, on the canvas of
    The present-day conundrum.
    My Achilles
    Tendencies,
    Your Achilles
    Tenderness,
    And the balance of
    Our complimentary opposites.
All vague titles
    For the abstract moving pictures
    That arrive
    In a moment of intended silence.
    I find myself
    Having been quite fine
    For some time,
    And wonder,
    Is that peace?
    Or just the ending of an aggravation…

We are all losers,
>   But can be
>   Equal
>   Through the losses
>   Just as much
>   As the triumphs.
>   To make ourselves giants
>   We forget the beauty
>   Of our smallness
>   And frequently use the wrong words
>   To define our wishes.
>   We ride the common complaint
>   In togetherness
>   And while struggling to
>   Under
>   Stand
>   We
>   Over
>   Diagnose.
>   I consciously say
>   We
>   Because I, myself,
>   Am tired of being so individual
>   And
>   Think it might be a good idea
>   To play with the other children.

There are days
    Where even words feel heavy.
    Pulled from the pit
    Of nothing at all,
    While entire body works
    To muster even the slightest sound.
    Feet of dumb weight
    Heave misguided bones
    To no end,
    Propelled by the desire
    To simply not be still.
    Anything, but that.
    The stillness, so thick as it is
    With the anger and stench
    That surrounds in dank humidity,
    Rendering the goodness of world
    So very unseeable.
    To clean my teeth,
    To lift my arm,
    To place my cup,
    To chew my breakfast,
    To answer your question,
    To think ahead,
    To swallow,
    Is too much.
    So heavy,
    Is the day.

A hook, for the crestfallen.
    A Life-line for the weak and laid out on floors.
    A simple affirmation, I too, am this way.
    An egoic exercise
    An egoic exorcise.
    My throat glides or stumbles, or crawls
    Over the map of the melody
    That is birthed by my heart.
    I believe in this primal something.
    I remain a convert of the religion of absolute insanity
    That can be the only thing that truly matters.
    It has to be.
    All of the rest of it is just dumb training for more of the rest of it.
    I see the way the world is working,
    And work to see the world, this way.
    This way is something to be proud of, maybe.
    This way, at least, is my way.
    And that is enough of a something
    To be proud of.

Why

Do they say,
She took her own life?
Where?
Or, and then did what with it?
How come
they say,
We lost someone?
As if they
Were just misplaced.
I see the older ones
Releasing their grief
In Sighs
And words.
In their shutting doors loudly
And anger at their jobs.
They narrow the corridors of their sadness
With dark liquid,
And hardly enough food.
It looks more like
They are the lost.
All this mess,
To resist
Shedding a tear.

I see the young kid planning
    And think;
    Please don't do it.
    You're too young to sell your soul.
    (As if there were an appropriate age.)
    Life consists
    Of choosing distractions
    And at the end, we weigh up
    Whether or not
    We chose the worthy ones.
    It's all so dull
    And beautiful
    And petty.
    Don't waste it on getting by.
    Don't get bogged down.
    Don't forget to forgive.
    Don't leave without saying goodbye.
    Don't only remember the bad parts.
    Don't keep your head high;
    Keep it wherever you want.
    We need you.
    We need you to show us again what we believed;
    That life is a stupid and beautiful mess,
    And snacks are enough to keep you burning.
    We think that nothing matters, and that's a horrible thing.
    Because we forget,
    That nothing matters, and that's a beautiful thing.

Please.
Don't give over to the ways of seeing
That litter our days
With crumbs of sadness.
I Don't want you to be hurt.
I don't want you to hate your body.
I don't want you to suffer unnecessarily.
I don't want the images to haunt you.
I don't want you to be persuaded.
I don't want you to give in.
I don't want my disease to be in your blood.
I don't want your anger to overcome you.
I don't want you to ever squash
Any part of yourself, or others.
I don't want you to cry over yourself.
I don't want them to get to you.
I don't want you to feel alone in it.
Your bodies are beautiful.
You deserve to know this.
You deserve to feel it.
These goals are sad and shameful.
Thin. Fit. Sexy. Optimal. Ideal.
Byproducts of hurt
By Products of hurt.
I'm tired of finding out,
That people hate themselves.
I'm going to try to tell you that
Everything is all nothing anyway,
So you might as well try my way.
Be violently you.
Allow that to change.
Allow the world that pleasure.
Don't do it.
We need you to see;

Your way.

Believe it, for flowers sake.
Believe it, for the crumb.
For the axe, for the ache.
Believe it, for the arm that's shaking
And too old to control itself.
For the lost and the frightened cry
Of a child too young to understand yet.
For the kids too scared to be themselves.
For the idea of ideas.
For the ones who have lost all hope.
That Love prevails and grace remains.
That humour heals, and talk is ecstatic.
That energy burns and fire gives heat.
Believe it; that thought so vague and unnerving;
It matters.

We are all
Bumbling about
Searching for the solution,
And probably we have the same reason
But see from different perspectives.
Working hard to be busy
With worthy, agreed-upon distractions
Like
Picking up rolls from bakeries
Or purchasing white goods
That save us time and effort
Which we fill with other types
Of time and effort.
We move in the common madness
Of this time, with effort,
And find brilliant and effective ways
Of eliminating the hurt from our brains,
And shit from our hearts.
We plumb our own souls
And have to learn to hold our own hands
As we stumble, trying to balance between them;
All of the things
We are taking with us.
I am always happy when I have found a comfortable way
To balance those things,
And manage to smoke a cigarette
At the same time.

#2

The willful forgetting
Of a suitcase.
He Died
Regrettably,
Unfortunately,
Slowly,
Humorously,
Silently,
Meaningfully.
Taken by shadowed, streamlined hands
And gently
Returned to the Archive.
He Moved through life
Collecting hello's
And goodbye's
And
In the end
The Goodbyes had it.
His intentions were noble.
Body, Solar powered.
A Life, well-lived.
A Death, Well handled.

Your tiny little spine
Makes me nervous.
Like I could cut myself,
If walking at speed
And accidentally too close.
Like small marbles
Stacked atop one another
Within a sack of soft silicon;
Those crane machines
Across the road from this place
Share a similar harsh angle.
I overhear nothing of your conversation,
Because I am sat too far away,
But nonetheless
Paint picture of you
On my medium-sized
technological device.
I take a large drink of water,
Then head around the corner
To where I work.
I can hear the marbles,
And am thankful I arrived early.

There is a phrase of condemnation
Resting on the tip of each tongue,
Aching for a suitable recipient.
We wrestle with our own bodies
While the constant work of confidence
Keeps us busy
With it's poison lists,
And for or against thinking.
We invented evil,
And remain repulsed.
We condemn wholeheartedly,
In order to separate.
We are optimistic,
And beautiful,
And kind,
But get so confused sometimes.
We get self righteous
And write poems about we,
Because
We don't know what else to do.

I was the clothing that dropped slowly
Off the corner of the table.
I was the harsh bit of criticism she gave
To an unwilling recipient,
And was carried for a long time
Before being let go.
I was that pause
Between those two words
You took, because you weren't sure
Whether to commit.
I am the current crop of what's to come
With potential that extends beyond my years.
I'm the heartfelt speech, that remains a note
On the 24th page of his notebook
Because the courage isn't there yet.
I get tossed aside, and hit the ankle of an older gentleman
Who has the desire, but not the back strength,
To pick me up.
I'll be waiting for the train when the news comes through.
I'll become the 255th person to utter the new cool phrase of the year.
I'll be the crease in the shirt of the new employee.
I'll be forgotten, and then remembered, And born anew.
I'll be the signal of a need for change.
I was born,
I am alive,
Take your time,
I'll be here for a while.

The dental floss of stillness
Dislodging the crumbs
From between the teeth
Of
day to day.
Our words are our words,
Their meaning;
Everybody else's.
I look up at the ink bleed
Of today's sky
And contemplate the routine
While playing with a hair that has grown too long.
I ask myself what others ask themselves,
And wonder how many of them are even asking at all.

Abstract, unknown, immeasurable.
A collection of letters used
To form a word
That encapsulates a thought
Which is
Driven by a feeling.
The complex web of who we are;
Whatever that means.
By whatever means
We formulate this illusion
Of a consistent I,
We continue to rely.
Trapped in the routine usness,
Because these are the functions
That I performs.
We break down, because we turn too often
On the same axis.
But to see ourselves
As the wheel in the first place,
Is the root of this unending paradox
Between wants and needs
And doing, and being.
What paradox?
What wrestle?
I see myself...

Consistency; the magnet
Of the chaotic mind.
Consistency; the saviour
Of the brutal madness within.
Consistency; the barrier
To the chaos and madness
That is, after all,
Living.

                                            The uncut vegetable,
That indicates the unquiet
And non-presence.
I'm following through man!
I'm nothing but that.
I'm nothing but getting things done.
I'm all about the one to the next
And the business of being busy.
Brave?
What happened.
Trying to be the gentle cog .
What happened?
Trying to be the one person who.
Trying to be a source
From which the goodness grows.
What happens
When "what happened?"
Doesn't answer a goddamn thing.

I skim the surface of a milk left sweating
$$\text{Like a fisherman biding his time}$$
$$\text{Before the big catch.}$$
$$\text{I simmer in the heated waters of my own}$$
$$\text{Petty problem.}$$
$$\text{I schedule a time, to schedule more time,}$$
$$\text{For unscheduled time.}$$
$$\text{I breathe in, but refuse to breathe out}$$
$$\text{And wonder why it all feels so restricted.}$$

The tight corset of my intentions to be good.
The fourth hole in my belt, still not tight enough.
Don't worry about me,
That would only provide me with what I'm asking for.
I don't need that.
I don't know what I need.
I need to make a change.
I need to remember to write it down.
I need to stand up,
In more ways than one.
I need to sit down,
And face the several contradictory sentences
At the forefront of my brain.
An organism, not an idea.
An organism, not an idea.
An organism, not an idea.

The diagonal finger, brushing lightly
Against the coldest plate.
Stroking with sensitivity and love;
The smooth edges of porcelain.
A window light over the left shoulder.
A wooden, four-legged table passed down and down;
The reflective top, mirroring the underlit face
Of a woman, caught up.
A dull butterfly wing fwippy fwap.
A Sadness, more mature in its old age.
More dignified in character.
This house is her home.
This home is her reminder.
She inhales.
She exhales.
A tender image painted awkwardly,
With words that will not quite do.

The laugh unattended to.
　　　　　　　　The echo that never came back.
　　　　　　　　The soreness of the right knee cap.
　　　　　　　　The excitement of a first kiss.
　　　　　　　　The solemnity of shared sickness.
　　　　　　　　The excuse that isn't good enough.
　　　　　　　　The stress that doesn't fly well.
　　　　　　　　The roundness of the rubber ball.
　　　　The height of the ceilings in her favourite building.
　　　　　　　　The sandwich too small.
　　　　　　　　The half is not enough.
　　　　　　　　The small squares of the universe.
　　　　　　　　The crossword of the day.
　　　　　　　　The what we see when we see finally;
　　　　　　　　　　　　　　　We are all in this together.

Spit information;
Too fast for the truth.
A Branch grown inward;
Nature's Misspelling.
It's okay to laugh;
It doesn't mean you're not sad.

Coward in the corner,
Cowered in the corner.
That Charm;
Simply
Stationary on the desk
Of my being.
The blunt edges;
Of some forgotten way of getting on
With others.
I light myself on fire
With such stale and dull repetition,
The flame feels cool.
I find myself, Lost.
I ask myself to stop talking.

Slimy and skilled
With pale facial features
                                                That rival the magazine crowd.
                                                         What printed paper?
                                                       What timeless artifact?
                                                   What loyalty to an idea?
                                                     The pearls sit untouched
                                              In the draw, opened frequently.
                      The seat by the window
                      That looks out on a dead street.
                      She doesn't remember getting here.
                      She doesn't remember why she came.
                          The pearls remain silent.
                            What youthful grin?
                            Whose bold ambition?
                          What loyalty to a dream?

The heart attack husband
Comes home late, to avoid the silence
Of what he's built.
There's a sharp kind of stillness
In that place.
I've never been happy to be asked to dine there.
What conversation?
What friendship?
What loyalty to loving?

The moon fell backwards and broke its left ankle;
Another fall,
Another eclipse.
The comma took charge, moved town,
And fired its literary agent;
Another life,
Another, purpose.
Someone fell from a third storey window around here and called the insurance company on the way down;
Another wail,
Another full stop.

Man bent over:
>Drinking from toilet sink.
>Hands cupped to receive
>And no time to wait.
>The water is all the same,
>After all.
>Man observing bent man
>Drinking from toilet sink:
>He came to a museum
>That was closed,
>But walked away with something to think about Anyway.
>The water is all the same,
>After all.

Bloated flower
Overweight with happiness.
I have wiped the shit from your hole
And examined the skin beneath your neck,
Looking everywhere
For something to explain
Where the beauty comes from.
I, in my inverse un-loveliness,
Send request
Through the unseen telephone line
That runs between us all
For the gift of similar garments.
Breaking the muscles of my weaker thought,
I prepare
For the someday, when
It will all be less heavy.
Floating through life
As a pair of lightweight scarves,
We'll share in the glow
And become the context
For new gifts,
Like
Two birthdays on the same day.

#3

My Face Came off
And fell into the sandpit
While waiting for my daughter to slide.
The imagery isn't original, nor mine,
But it's the best I have right now.
I wonder when I'll be myself again;
Dissatisfied with a man
Who can only bend down several times,
Before wanting to go home.
I know I belong with you,
On that slide,
But Life is tiring.
I'll help you back up,
But we must be going soon.
Why?
You're not quite ready to ask that of me yet
But when you do,
I won't have a good enough answer.

Stale Crease,
Belief.
Sat up politely, he ordered
The cheapest thing on the menu,
To see what it would feel like
To live that way.
She drew a circle, that
Wasn't a circle
(But I'm not going to tell her that)
For the sake of love.
The next-door neighbours
House children who scream
(Because - good on them)
To the judgement
Of the man sitting politely.
I look into the eyes
Of the one who drew the circle,
And vow;
Never to dampen her screaming;
For the sake of love.

                        I was recently asked how my mind works,
              And thought; I'm not sure that it does.
                    Our uniquely human
                        Indirectness
                        Breeds some

Intangible affinity
With what isn't,
But
May...be.
But...

                                              Maybe
                               The grey hairs
                                 were correct
                               In their pursuit
                                  Of simplicity.
                    I'll think on it a while longer,
                          And remain unsure.

It all seems so complicated to me.

To hitch a ride
With you
Is a religious experience,
Heavy set motorcycle man.
You used to be so angry
Stuck in the day to day.
You tell me you weren't happy
Until tragedy
And cancer
Collaborated
To Take your family
And your idea of what happens in life,
Away.
Forcing you to figure out some other manner
Of being.
You say it was hard,
With such casualty
That only wisdom
Acquired through immense pain
Would allow.
Your ex wife,
The distant niece of confucius,
Doesn't know who she left behind.
I leave inspired
Heavy set motorcycle guru man.
My thankyou
Rides the wind.

Well baby,
I think I hear you crying.
I thought that idea you had the other day
Was a good one,
And you should try and remember
That good ideas do come.
And people notice them from time to time.
Poor baby,
                        Your crying is a thick mass
                           On the other side of the wall.
              I know if I asked, you'd only change the subject.
"It's the good kind of cry" you'd say.
As if you should be thankful
For the pain.
Maybe you should baby,
I don't know.
I know that much.
All I know is how to be here.
So all I can offer, is my being here,
And hope, you don't wish I was someone else.
Baby,
                        I hope you don't wish you were someone else,
                  Because I'm "being here", on the other side of this wall,
                        And I wouldn't have you any other way.

I smile when I open my door
And see the traffic controllers,
From afar.
Because,
They are like my friends now,
In this new place where I have left my others behind.
They always clear a space for me
And offer their kindness
In daily how are you's.
Our bond is close
And true.
I sometimes think, I should really
Invite them to a dinner party at my house,
But I'm scared the relationship will strain
In the light of a foreign context.
It will be unfortunate,
If the conversation cannot get past
How hot the day was
And embarrassing,
If we can't help but occupy our usual roles.
They might feel compelled
To part the guests around me, when I cross to the Bathroom.
Or
I might unnecessarily shout,
As if speaking from the other side of the street.
For now,
I think,
It is enough to laugh with each other,
In between traffic.

Darling small one.
Your father picks odd things up from the ground.
Your mother keeps an unusual amount of glass jars.
Your father is prone to getting too wrapped up in his own head.
Your mother, her own heart.
Your father complains a lot.
Your mother listens.
Your mother feels a lot but struggles to put it into words.
Your father listens to the silences and helps where he can.
You will have great moments.
You will have moments that make you forget the great ones ever existed.
You will be shocked at how little you mean to others.
You will be shocked at how much you mean to others.
You will be surprised at who remembers your name.
You will be hurt
You will develop ways to cope.
You will feel unbelievably happy
And may spend restless years trying to grasp
The source of that happiness.
You will eventually learn, it's best not to think about it.
Your father loves you
Your mother loves you
Darling small one,
One day you might be walking,
Using your own grown legs
To transport your own grown body along the path
And
Perhaps you will stop to sit down at some coffee shop, and have some time in your own company
As I am doing now.
You might Smile.
You may even laugh to yourself,
Knowing all of these things.

What does it matter?
I ask myself, as if it mattered what mattered.
We're all drunk
On something
And constantly making plans
To see each other
Next time.

                                          The pale shirts,
                    With their university degrees in trauma
                                Are walking around
                        With their certificates of sadness
                              Taped to their chest.

The little big people
Are making rules like cups of coffee
And getting high
From the smell
                    Of their own darkness.
                My ego; the bitter little bastard,
                        Went on strike
But
He was the moneymaker
And now I'm head poor,
And heart heavy.
I'm Sober as anything
And missing the illusion
Of mattering.

I take ownership
Of these unwanted private thoughts,
And have learned
That not everyone is available for a coffee at all times.
One in two of us
Is considering suicide seriously
And I'm left wondering
If it is you or me.
I see the most amazing crumbs
On this brilliant humming earth,
Fighting to justify their separation from the sandwich
And remain quiet, slightly to one side,
Wanting better things for them.
I feel the worst often,
And the best occasionally,
Which is just enough
To keep going.
Everything in this world
Is true and untrue,
But I know for certain
That we can still learn
From the people who are no longer with us
And
Some American music
Still holds the power, to calm us down.

I get up early
To fit things in
Because when the others are awake,
It's not the same thing;
The world changes with witness.
It shifts in its seat.
It puts on a clean shirt.
I take note of the skipped heartbeat in my chest
And move my thoughts slightly to the left.
We avoid it.
We make excuses and reschedule our plans with it.
We climb ladders to be taller than it.
We inflate our inner balloons to decorate the party of it.
We try to get a grip on it.
We keep trying,
All in an effort to be bigger.
Bigger than our pain.

MY DAUGHTER ON FIRE

You hit the side of my shoulder
Because you don't know what else to do.
You feel something that you can't define,
Because language hasn't reached those parts yet.
The primal inner urgency that bloats and swells
Your tiny little rib cage,
Fills you up.
You haven't yet learned
Of poking holes in your heart
So the steam can get out.
I don't know If I'm doing the best by you,
But all I can do is show you what I know.
Maybe that's why you struggle.
Because I struggle.
We can go through this together.
We can share a moment over breakfast,
And you can teach me how to plug the holes
I learned to poke,
So we can feel through this thing,
Together.

I stare at the socket.
I become the bridge between the wound
And the wanting.
Sometimes, I realize,
It is about collaborating with the difficulty of the day
To find the morsels of light
I keep standing in front of.
To find the light,
To find your light.
I seek acceptance in the bottom
Of an empty cup.
I refill myself in preparation of the needs
Of tomorrow,
Forgetting about the needs of now;
Which are not always to be refilled.
I need to find the light.
I need to reassess the posture
And keep calm in this dance.
I need to breathe.

This season of sadness.
So dull was the evening
You cried into my shirt,
Because it feels so normal to me now.
Wednesday's tears.
									I see the tooth marks That burn red
											In your hot little hand,
Born from a special brand of discomforted anger that cannot be un-
												derstood,
											And think;
										Except by me.
					I see it in you.
					My heaviness. My fear. My violence.
					My dear, I have spent the year screaming;
							Why?
						Is this the will of the wind?
					Does a quarter-turn of this dumb giant rock
								Knock everything slightly to the wrong?
									I am absolutely floored by it.
									I am absolutely on the floor from it.
										This season of sadness.

I remember the smell of the rain
And the red and blue top-shirt
With an unused breast pocket.
I remember feeling young,
And my thoughts directed at thighs
Or rounded belly, which filled me
With such dread, a burger felt like a mountain.
I remember feeling so much.
Too much.
I remember those tiny decisions, made thoughtlessly,
That eventually lead to here.
I miss the boy.
I miss the tears.
I miss the aching and the satchel bag,
Covering my insecure body.
I miss the cigarettes after school
And the hope of being a giant in this place.
I find my sight unaimed.
I look for more.
I hear myself thinking
Instead of living.
I miss the boy.

The towel was still wet
Due to
Inadequate tucking

And In that simple moment
I felt the hole of my unevenness.
I felt the presence
Of the lack of presence
Of you.
        Your tucking of my inadequately tucked
            Things
          Keeps me upright. Keeps me alive.
            Keeps me going.
I need you.
I Love you.
I'm sorry for the ways I act to the contrary;
Knowing you know it, despite them.
I am thankful for the strength and patience,
That allows you
To love a mad man.

I'm not paranoid,
                      I'm just cautious.
                    But,
           Maybe that's the wrong word.
Maybe they'll read that and use it against me,
Somehow.
I say somehow, because they're cunning.
                They, being the ones inside
              Who keep me on the defense,
            Staring at my own back.
I took up the role when I was young
And haven't looked back since,
Except the ongoing looking back,
Previously mentioned.
I'm not paranoid,
I'm just...careful.

#4

18 AND OVER

But
Not at least this tall to ride.
[Closed Caption Applause]
The sound of a thought let go.
[Closed Caption Gasp]
My knuckle cracking to a room of quiet employees
[Closed Caption Silence]
The subtle drop of a left shoulder, indicating unease.
[Closed Caption Self-Consciousness]
A room full of No's.
[Closed Caption Yes]
The crust of the bread.
[Closed Caption The End]
[Closed Caption Ellipses]

The fifth grade performance of
"The little prayer" Began 15 minutes late, because Leonard put his pants on backwards.
The pants were not important.
The lights came up at 6:15 on 12 panicked little expressions,
And Mary was the first to speak.
The singing was somewhat in unison, but the script was lackluster.
I couldn't help from drifting off in the second act, when the assumed
Protagonist began his journey back to normalcy, and the "Tree"
At the back of the stage fell over.
The choice to use colour-coated clothing was somewhat inspired,
But beyond the occasional moments of stylistic proficiency
I was left unimpressed.
I was excused from being in the play myself, because it was felt
That my presence may be too powerful, and may take away
From my other classmates.
I'm not bitter, I'm disappointed.
The play ended 15 minutes late; at 7:45, and I was left with nothing but my desire for dessert to think about.
The character development was non-existent,
The lighting was too dark,
The music was almost always out of key
And I can tell you one thing for certain;
If I was that tree, I would not have fallen over.

SLOW FADE INTO...
"ROGER BUDGE"
The soap salesman from Minnesota
And main guru
Of some new kind of enlightenment.
Off-script, roger removes the gum from his shoe as we
ZOOM INTO:
His filthy tie.
THE VOICE OVER BEGINS...
(Side note: Roger refused to speak on set due to crippling self-consciousness relating to his front left lateral incisor, and so we, the audience, must assume the voice belongs to him.)
CONTINUED...
"With my unique tools, everybody always finds what they want
Without ever needing to realize
They are wanting in the first place!
Why?
Because they are HAVING! Not wanting.
In just 36 hours I'll teach you how to expertly replace wanting, with HAVING!!!
You'll learn how to beat those pesky unhappy feelings to the punch,
And remain happy forever" (Or at least the next few hours.)
CROSS DISSOLVE:
Roger is sitting on the arm of a bench, despite the bench being empty.
"I'm sitting here not because I WANT to, but because I HAVE to."
ROGER SMILES and after a little longer than necessary...winks.
His dumbly formed joke hangs in the minds of our unsuspecting audience as we
QUICKLY FADE OUT.

DIG
The way the heat does nothing for your toes, but everything for your torso.
INVITE the rest of your abandoned sentence back to the house, for a coffee you already wish was over.
BELIEVE the pale footed sous chef
Who prays with both hands lifted
To gods who retired years ago.
HEAR HIM; They warned, and explained, and filled out all the appropriate paperwork,
But when you get to a certain age, people stop listening.
RETIRE your need to climb above the little ones and
LEARN that all the best angles are at eye level or below.
ARRIVE having eaten, but continue to eat in the name of politeness.
INVEST your money in time; the only stock worth anything.
DO not be more afraid than is biologically necessary.
BELIEVE
BELIEVE
BELIEVE
You me.

(SOMEWHERE NONSPECIFIC)
THE CURTAIN OPENS...
Beside exterior laundrette, a young boy delivers Coffee
Shaking like a wet noodle.
PICTURE:
Customers Sitting,
All aligned in lines
Like hollow croissants.
The Fragile Pastry of their own delicate selves
Crumbles beneath their feet,
As they wait
For their own brand of Jam
(Or Cheese or cream or whatever)
To help fill the hole.
MEANWHILE...
It is rumoured:
Six doctors have swallowed a lego head,
The Bee died of guilt,
And the girl divorced her parents.
As it goes,
More things seem to need to be done
These days.
For whatever reason,
The clocks turn for well-dressed men
And the paralytic dance goes on.
BACK AGAIN...
We leave the scene wherever it is,
Never to be seen, from this angle again.
CUT TO:
Hollow croissant.

The Boy had ambition.
At the tender age of six, he had already
Established himself as a political heavyweight and social activist.
The self-appointed mayor of his own street,
He enlisted the help of neighbouring children
To clean up "This one horse town"
As he put it, having recently overheard the phrase
In a film.
One weekend, he proposed the project
Of a charity pancake drive
And enlisted the help of local investors (Mr and Mrs Mother and Father)
To cover the cost of ingredients and administration duties.
He demanded a budget of twelve dollars,
And spent the bulk of it in a week
On multicoloured paper clips,
And goes at the hammer game.
With the big day approaching
And with no pancakes to show for himself,
He plead the fifth
And played to his parent's maternal instincts
By claiming he'd been robbed at plastic gunpoint on his way to the shops.
The jury, (Mostly made up the friends that bore witness to his crime)
Turned on their mayor.
Having grown frustrated with his leadership techniques,
The 12 angry boys took no time at all to arrive at their verdict:
"GUILTY OF MISAPPROPRIATION OF FUNDS AND OF GENERALLY BEING NO FUN TO PLAY WITH."
They proposed the death penalty as punishment.
Judges mother and father, deciding that such a course of action may be a little harsh,
Exercised their discretion and sentenced him instead
To one week,

Without television.

UPDATE:
The boy has not yet grown up
And is currently still paying off his debt by washing dishes and taking out the trash.
He is apologetic and deeply regretful of his actions
And hopes to one day return to politics.

My mother was a strict, steely woman.
The most passionate advice she ever gave was
Never, Ever,
Fall in love with a Tenor.
They'll spend their entire lives,
And all the families money
Fighting their way up the musical ladder.
Higher and higher up the scales,
And further away from the relationship.
And believe me,
They always want help getting down.
He will have has his way with you,
Consume your womanhood during the intermission,
And toss you aside, Before the encore.
Precious child,
If you simply cannot escape
The seductive magnetism
Of the musical breed,
Please, I implore You,
At least find yourself a nice, humble
Bagpipe player.

In the world;
Location unknown,
Two fish and chip boys
With their chicken pock scars
Sit getting their haircut by the bowling ball barber
And trading stories of the all the women,
They've never really met.
Across the street,
A young man who took out a loan to purchase his morning coffee,
Is struggling under the weight
Of his parent's expectations.
Nearby,
The sweet-natured traffic controller
Gives wise advice on healing wounds
With Honey and spiders-webs.
In walking distance,
An old woman says out loud to no one,
"The earth comes together under the threat of bad weather"
And
A small group of dapperly dressed people
Sigh, and get back to work.
In a moment,
Everyone on earth
Will take a breathe at the same time,
But nobody will notice.

Last night we were strangers.
I had lost you to the cavernous landscape
                                          Of the Queen-sized bed.

Cold and Unafraid, I hiked for hours
Trying to find my way back
To the cradle of your tender limbs.
                        For weeks I swam
                    Beneath the far-reaching hills
                      of Merino cotton.
On my travels, I came across a shaman,
Who told the tale
Of the best Jam that money could by.
              I overcame demons, summoned all my strength
                And fought through the supermarket aisles
                    Of my subconscious
                  For that Jam.
                          I felt, deep within my dreaming bones
                            That I needed to gift you this Jam
                                When we woke up,
                                  In time for breakfast.
                It took me years, but I found you.
            In the delicate squish of unaware,
              You lay your head on my chest,
                Which had aged Overnight.
There, lying in the foggy awakening of cling-film eyes
We met, Exhausted and pleased,
As the day began.

Victor wraps his head
Around the events of the day.
First,
He caught the 618 bus,
And stared at the man in camouflage
Who was still able to be seen, in the seat beside him.
Then
He walked 500 metres to the beach
And realized he'd forgotten the sunscreen.
After
Ten minutes of doing his daily crossword
He lost his pen to the volleyball king,
who needed it to keep score.
One hour later,
Sans pen,
He shuffled his way to the coffee shop on the corner
And ordered Two poached eggs,
Which never came.
After 46 minutes,
He paid for the meal he didn't receive
And walked back to the Bus stop.
Finally,
He caught the 618 bus back home
And stared at the empty seat beside him,
Wondering if there was anyone there.

Wheaties,
Spilled like stale confetti on the pale linoleum floor
Of the supermarket.
The rounded son of tolerant mother refuses to go to
Space camp.
Rows and rows of cheerios, The only witness to his crime.
Unaware of onlooking cereal
The boy sobs
A secret sob.
He is afraid because in fact
He wants to go to space camp so much,
He cannot handle his own enthusiasm.
This sensitive boy will go on to be called a sissy
For crying too much.
He will learn that being too sensitive
Is no good in this life.
He will shed his weight and with it, his space-loving, plump, heart.
The cheerios, knowing all too well How the story goes,
Begin to cry also.
Soon, Someone will complain,
And they will need to be restocked
On account
Of being too soggy
To sell.

JESUS STICKER.

I Walk into school
Looking like a jesus sticker,
And pray to myself
For all the drama of midday television.
I lap that shit up, like the dried-out dog that I am.
The stoop fucks keep their shirts untucked
As if it's some big revelation.
The oily haired dropkick kitty gang spit shit on people's shoes,
To prove their bullshit rebellion.
My teacher's think i'm more intelligent than the effort I put it.
Which doesn't make any sense and will probably harm me in later life.
Thick bastards.
Jane left her lunch at home
But she doesn't give a fuck.
What a chick.
She borrows a sandwich from grace.
I say borrow, because she never keeps it down
For long.
I remember
Purposely falling in pools at parties
To give these fools something to remember.
Something to pluck the brutal string of nostalgia
When they're in their mid-40's, and missing the good old days
When that god like jesus looking guy accidentally fell into the pool that one time.
"Nobody accidentally falls into pools anymore" they'll think, with sorrow,
Not knowing
That nobody ever did.
And it's all just a carousel of agreement.
Someone fucked someone,
Someone said something,
Someone took something.

We all just believe it matters.
And that's why It does,
And later,
Doesn't.
And here I am, getting ahead of myself
Like I always do.
Thinking too much,
And missing out on the fun shit.

Marcy and The Smooth Oak Fisherman.

Her days flew by like small excursions when she was with The Smooth Oak Fisherman.

The Smooth Oak Fisherman whose broad shoulders Presented a barrier to anyone wanting to get through any of the same doors. The Smooth Oak fisherman, who smelled of yesterday's flowers and tasted of foreign fruit. She recalls often feeling like time had stood still.

Probably because The Smooth Oak Fisherman moved so slowly he was often mistaken for a still frame. Marcy, who had tried her best to play the role of tiny companion,

Soon found her infatuation with the hulking beauty quickly crumbled

Beneath the weight of his own chi chi chin. She grew weary and homesick for herself.

Of afternoon sunsets, he would tell her of how the twilight matched itself to the colour of her pale complexion and spoke of the many offered pleas he'd turned down for the here and now. She eventually noticed The Smooth oak fisherman was inclined to the over usage of recently learned words and for a large part of their time together, he reused the observations that everything is fallacious, and the sky was a beautiful shade of ultramarine. One afternoon while observing The Smooth Oak Fisherman ponder the vastness of life, she realised that his massive, eternally furrowed brow painted him less as deep in thought, and more as a child, struggling to read a difficult sentence.

In one fail swoop, she broke the Smooth Oak Fisherman's boat sized heart

And left, to return to the life she'd abandoned in return for a shot at a life she'd thought she wanted, but soon discovered, she didn't.

Brooding and confused, The Smooth Oak fisherman became paralysed and fell silent,

Into a vaccum of nothingness, where he still resides, to this day.

I tell you this tale dear reader, in an effort to warn you. That If you should ever find yourself atop a particularly broad mountain and smelling the tender scent of yesterday's flowers, be careful not to slip.

You may, in fact,

Be atop a Smooth Oak Fisherman.

Mrs Brampton
Will appear
In Crouch theatre's Production of
"Snob Johnsons day off"
Tomorrow evening,
In the role of "Mrs Snob Johnson".
Mrs Brampton succeeds Annie Farraway in the part,
Who sails for London on wednesday
To once again, start a new life
As someone else.
The aforementioned play
Is remarkably tiresome
And
The director's use of a Ham sandwich
As metaphor for the modern condition,
Leaves much to be desired.
The only genuine pleasure
Is the moment
The curtain finally closes.
Once again, this reviewer
Is left questioning
His life choices.
Wishing Annie Farraway,
Smooth sailing.

The Small policeman is always alert.
Making use of his stature
To outsmart the taller ones.
"Something for everyone"
He is taken to say, of an evening
At after work drinks.
Only,
The words come from too far down
To reach anyone.
They mistake him
For a sad man.
Must be,
At a height like that.
But
They are half the man
He is,
And he is at least twice
The half man, he appears.
He picks up the laughs
That fall on the ground,
And tries again.

The cheap man
Saves on everything.
Cutting down on conversation
To stockpile for a rainy day.
Choosing only
From the bargain bin of thoughts
Within his brain.
One day,
He will meet the one meant for him,
And spoil her with his wisdom and wit.
Having saved enough for years of intelligent discussion,
They will Parley from noon to dusk,
And it will eventually drive her mad.
He will wish he'd spent his thoughts more wisely
And realize, his metaphors no longer apply.
She will teach him to value the shorter sentence,
And be rid of lengthy digressions.
He will donate his funds to the youth, who have more years of discussion to fill.
They will talk it out,
Move on,
And Live happily,
Without worrying.

All these women,
Having broad brunches,
Talking of things
As if they don't matter.
Heavy cheese,
Breaking cracker in half
To save face,
Because Susanne is on a diet,
And one mustn't be seen
To love oneself too much.
A long life
Of slender proportions,
And never quite enough.
When the cheque arrives,
Jennifer suddenly needs consoling.
Susanne is sneaking Pâté
Between the sobs,
And the cheque waits awkwardly,
Careful not to interrupt.

THE GIFT.
Someone...
Left a piece of rubbish in my letterbox.
Addressed to me.
You sick, beautiful thing.
You knew it would delight me.
My mind Is tingling, with possibilities.
Oh, joyful why!
Exquisite where!
Profound who!
Did you purchase it, with wicked intention?
You devilish beast.
I love the thought of you dancing down the aisle, full of giddy purpose.
Paying over the counter with sinful pride of kept secret.
Did you drive home or did you walk?
Maybe you caught the bus, and gazed out the window with longing.
Maybe it helps to calm you.
Did you get home to an empty house, because your husband or wife was away for the weekend?
Or still at work?
Perhaps you live alone, peculiar creature.
Children?
Maybe you unfolded the crucial part your plan in plain sight! Surrounded on all sides.
I like to think of you sitting at your dining table,
Consuming it's contents with duty.
Extracting the bowels and removing the internal organs with the precision of a surgeon.
You rid the vessel of its unnecessary parts and reveal it's true form.
One of Mangled mystery.
Crumpled and contorted,
Pure
in it's Trashiness.
Washing your grotty little hands.

Brushing your offensively crooked smile.
Ridding your body of pedestrian outfit, and turning off the light.
Every morning that begins with the thought of garbage
Is a good one.
I bet you handled it with care, as if it were a piece of high art.
It is to me.
You know your audience so well.
This all important gesture,
Will occupy prime position
On the walls of my mind,
In the museum of my head.
Bravo.
I thank you,
Sick
beautiful
Superb being
For this marvellous gift.
I Love you,
You loathsome thing.
Happy valentines day.

Instructions for a moment of utter despair:

In the extreme case of total destruction, please refrain from any swift movements or loud screaming. If resistance has truly become futile, these actions will do nothing to serve you.

We suggest a brief trip down memory lane to pay respect to your loved ones and cherished past-times. Once this is completed, we ask that you do your best to sit as quietly and comfortably as you can, in the Inevitability of your coming demise. As always we offer a complimentary snack with your choice of tea or coffee. We hope you enjoy your time with us today and trust you have a pleasant Journey. Please don't hesitate to let the cabin crew know if we can assist you in any other way.

She sees through you
Diabetic Beer man,
Like a bad amber ale.
You do your best to cloak the intention of your inquiries
In the smoke of erroneous questions,
But you give yourself away
Everytime you say that word.
Your wife joins you,
Beer?
The lovely patient Chemist plays along.
Of course, of course...Beer?
She tells you not to worry.
Thank you so much...and about the Beer?
P. Chem, As I will now call her,
Diligently summarizes the facts.
This medication will help balance your blood sugar
And that is the important part of this conversation.
Also it should be fine.
Beer!
You dance in the relief
Of the narrowly escaped tragedy
And praise your gods for their blessings of fortune.
I watch you leave
Oh Diabetic Beer couple,
Glowing with the knowledge
That beer is able to play a part in all of this.
I collect my Asthma medication,
Say my goodbyes to P.Chem,
And step outside for a cigarette.

THIS IS THE END OF THE BOOK.

THIS IS SOME STUFF ABOUT THE AUTHOR:

THOMAS CALDER IS A MULTIDISCIPLINARY CREATIVE WITH OVER 15 YEARS OF EXPERIENCE IN THE WORLDS OF MUSIC, FILMMAKING, PHOTOGRAPHY AND WRITING.

HIS JOURNEY IN THE CREATIVE INDUSTRIES STARTED AT A VERY YOUNG AGE; HAVING GROWN UP IN A CREATIVE FAMILY. ALWAYS FASCINATED WITH DISCOVERING NEW FORMS OF TELLING STORIES AND EXPLORING THE DEPTH OF HUMAN CHARACTER AND EMOTION - THOMAS'S LOVE OF POETRY AND PROSE WAS A NATURAL EXTENSION OF THIS IN-BUILT CURIOSITY.

FROM SELF-WRITING AND RECORDING HIS DEBUT ALBUM AT THE AGE OF 21, TO TOURING THE WORLD, WITH HIS MUSIC, MAKING FILMS, AND ESTABLISHING ANOTHER SUCCESSFUL CAREER IN THE WORLD OF PHOTOGRAPHY - THOMAS IS AN ARTIST WHO HAS NO BOUNDARIES WHEN IT COMES TO FORMS OF EXPRESSION.

A BRIEF TIMELINE:

26/07/1990:
BORN

26/07/1990 --NOW:

A WHOLE BUNCH OF STUFF; GROWING UP, LIVING, TOURING, WRITING MUSIC, MAKING FILMS, TAKING PHOTOGRAPHS, DRINKING COFFEE, TAKING WALKS, GIVING HUGS, BECOMING A FATHER, WRITING POEMS, FALLING OVER, MAKING THOUSANDS OF BREAKFASTS, ENJOYING COUNTLESS BOOKS, FILMS, ETC (AND MUCH MORE)

THIS MINUTE :
WRITING THIS TIMELINE.

THE FUTURE:
WHO KNOWS.

www.ingramcontent.com/pod-product-compliance
Lightning Source LLC
Chambersburg PA
CBHW020329010526
44107CB00054B/2044